My Genes Made Me Do It!

Moral Education, Charlotte Mason, and the New Genetics

James C. Peterson, PhD

Deani Van Pelt, PhD, series editor

CHARLOTTE
MASON
INSTITUTE

Series editor: Deani Van Pelt
Copy editors: Angie McCauley and Janelle Mills
Book/cover design and typesetting: Sharon Schnell, Terri Shown, Jody E. Skinner

This multi-authored monograph series, commissioned in connection with the Charlotte Mason Centenary, is designed to highlight and explore the continuing educational and leadership relevance of the late 19th-century British educationalist Charlotte Mason (1842–1923) through the collective contributions of the Armitt Museum and Library, the University of Cumbria, the Charlotte Mason Institute, and other scholars and practitioners worldwide.

Foreword

to the Charlotte Mason Centenary Series

Fewer than three decades ago a global surge of interest in the educational ideas of Charlotte Mason would have been unimaginable. Yet today, the design for education proposed by this late 19th and early 20th century educationalist is taking hold and influencing the teaching and learning of thousands of students and educators worldwide.

When we began discussing this series in early 2020, we sensed the potential of renewed scholarly focus on the writings and practices proposed by Charlotte Mason (1842-1923) but we did not anticipate how quickly the interest in her approach would be accelerated. The pandemic disruption of traditional classroom-based learning—and subsequent time spent exploring and experiencing alternatives—has resulted in many parents, teachers, students, school leaders, and policymakers, asking probing foundational questions—with unprecedented urgency and passion—about education.

With thousands of searches landing on the ideas of

Charlotte Mason and so many schools, homeschools, and educational cooperatives now being started around her philosophy and practices, this multi-authored series release is aptly timed. In it, a diversity of researchers, scholars, and practitioners have come together around one question: *what is the enduring legacy and relevance of Charlotte Mason for education today?*

The Centenary Series is a collaboration among the Charlotte Mason Institute, the Armitt Museum and Library, and the University of Cumbria. It was birthed as a project of the university's Charlotte Mason Studies program which, through its appointments of Visiting Research Fellows, results in international collaborative research, writing, and conferencing, that connects Charlotte Mason's legacy with education today.

The monograph you hold in your hand is one of eighteen, written by a diverse group of education professors, researchers, classroom teachers, parents, and priests from Canada, the USA, and the UK. Their widely varied backgrounds, experience, and areas of expertise offer readers different lenses through which Mason might be viewed today. We believe that taking this broad approach is an important step in bringing Mason's ideas into the realm of mainstream discourse.

The series includes monographs that address Mason's biography and offer inviting overviews of her educational theory. Some offer a more philosophical, theological, historical, moral, or anthropological analysis, while others delve deeply into specific aspects of pedagogy such as narration, living books, outdoor education, assessment, or nature journaling. Each draws on the intersection of the author's field and an aspect of Mason's biography or philosophy and practice.

We hope that this series will stimulate further research and study of key relevant Mason principles and practices for learning, education, and development today. In one sense, the series optimizes and capitalizes on Ambleside as a critical place—an international hub—for the research and study of Mason. On the Ambleside campus of the University of Cumbria, one experiences the place where Mason lived and worked from 1894-1923. Within the Armitt Museum's collection, located at the base of the Ambleside campus, one finds the Charlotte Mason Collection featuring documents and artifacts from Mason and the institutions she founded. Indeed, each monograph includes at least one artifact from the Armitt Collection and, with sufficient notice, is available for public access. In another sense, this series recognizes that Mason's ideas have again taken hold across the world with international scholars and educators making her ideas their own and enriching the lives and experiences of children everywhere, most of whom will never step foot in Ambleside. Thus, while

Ambleside is a natural destination for understanding and exploring Mason, it is hoped that this series will encourage more widespread study and engagement and continued conversation about the ideas of Mason's potentially vitalizing approach to relational education.

The Charlotte Mason Institute, with its long relationship with the Armitt and with the Ambleside Campus of the University of Cumbria, has generously contributed to this project through its role as publisher. CMI saw the promise in convening a wide variety of experts and has been an encouragement throughout. Our deepest gratitude goes to Prof. Lois Mansfield, Campus Director of the Ambleside Campus of the University of Cumbria, without whose tenacious vision, neither this project nor the other appointments and events that accompany its release would have happened. Faye Morrisey, Manager and Curator at The Armitt Museum and Library, was a tireless supporter of this project, ever ready to encourage the authors and editors and provide ready access to documents and artifacts when needed. Jody Skinner, Terri Shown, Sharon Schnell, Angie McCauley and Janelle Mills have generously provided endless support with layout, cover design, and copy editing. This project would not have come to be without their continuous persistent dedication. Kristen Forney's administrative support was invaluable as a project of this scale contains so many moving components. Our peer reviewers and project advisors were integral to this series and we are grateful for the privilege of working with so many kind and insightful colleagues in the field. My sincerest thanks to Hilary Cooper and Sally Elton-Chalcraft for encouraging this series and for their support throughout.

And finally, none of this would have been possible without our authors and all those who supported each one giving them time and space to research and write. These authors were a joy to work with and their contributions add significantly to the research and analysis offered on the relevance of Charlotte Mason's design for education today. We look forward to the questions, insights, and renewal of education practice, that their words will provoke.

Deani Van Pelt, PhD
Series Editor
June 2023
Ottawa, Canada

Abstract

Genes deeply shape each person's body and behavior, but they do not fully determine either. Human beings are sufficiently complex to make choices about what genetic tendencies to implement, and if so, how and when. It is fitting then to teach in a way that best connects with and builds upon each child's individual capacities and temperament, without being limited to merely the student's or teacher's first inclinations. We have genuine choice in how we channel genetic influence and so are able to shape who we become. Developing practiced virtues of well-focused attention and self-motivation are valuable for education and the rest of life. They are best recognized, emulated, and practiced out of joyful relationship with the source of all that is good.

Contents

List of Figures

Introduction

It is interesting that Charlotte Maria Shaw Mason had many half-siblings who were teachers, and both her grandparents and great-grandparents were principals of schools. Being raised by teachers or related to them does not mean that one will be a teacher. But it may indicate innate skills, inclinations, models, and opportunity to follow that course. This is the way of human genetics. It can enable and encourage, but to the degree that it predestines, it means that one will be substantially free. Our genes move us toward a particular physique, intellect, and behavior, but do not determine what we do with those starting points. We hear people say "My genes made me do it. I could not stop it. I am not responsible." Or more theologically, "My genes made me do it, and since God gave me my genes, that must be what I should do." But actually, the formative role of human genetics is quite a bit more complex than that.

What Genes Do for Structure and Behavior

Your eye is an intricate wonder. Given some time, a good laboratory, and some help, do you think you could make a human eye? You would have to get the right chemistry for the transparent but tough cornea lens, and shape it so that it focuses entering light precisely on the retina. Then you would need to form an optic nerve to carry the resulting data to the part of the brain structured to make sense of the gathered information. It is an overwhelmingly complex task, and yet you are reading this book, which indicates that you have probably made a human eye before. Maybe even two. So how did you do that?

All the instructions for how to make a human eye—the chemistry of its materials, its structure, its assembly—are written in your genes. In fact, not only do you have a complete set of instructions for your entire body inside each one of your nucleated cells—since you have about three billion nucleated cells in your body, you carry three billion complete sets of genes that each have all the required information to make your body. The recipes for heart and lung tissue, bone and sinew, brain cells and touch sensors, and how they all relate to each other are written in the necessary detail to establish form and function.

And these genes do not just direct the formation of

your body. If you turn on the light late at night in the kitchen and a cockroach is revealed on the floor, it will run for cover. How does it know to flee the light? That behavior is built into its genes. Its genetic code includes operating instructions. If it did not have that built-in behavior, it would not live long enough to pass its genes on to another generation of cockroaches. Without genetically encoded guides to behavior, birds would not know to fly south for the winter. Mammals would not know how to find mates or shelter.

People have operating instructions built into our genes too. They are not as rote as those for an insect, but still quite present. Already in the 1990s, a whole series of studies linked various aspects of temperament to particular inherited genetic codes such as for novelty seeking. When you go to a restaurant, do you always order your favorite or do you look to see if there is anything new to try? If the latter is more your inclination, you likely have a genetically encoded temperament to seek novelty (Ebstein et al., 1996). Some people, when suddenly confronted in a slide show with a picture of a human face that is showing fear, will have a stronger reaction than others (Lesch et al., 1996). Their bodies will instantly ready for action, such as by quickening their pulses. That is an inclination toward anxiety that can be quite helpful in some situations, but distracting or even harmful in others. In many cases, it is possible to predict a person's likely temperament from patterns in their genes.

Acknowledging this is not to fall into the old mistake of reductionism, or what is often called "nothing-buttery." Say a physicist is looking at a particular atom. She can describe the interaction of protons, neutrons, and electrons, even including the detail of subatomic particles. The description may be quite accurate. But then along comes a chemist who says that such is all well and good, but the collection of protons and electrons that we are observing is structured together as a molecule that we call glucose. There is a level of complexity present that the physicist did not describe. Then a biochemist shows up and says, "Well that's a good description of the basic molecule, but the glucose is part of a chemical reaction that releases power. We biochemists call it an ATP reaction." You have to know your biochemistry to recognize that part of what is actually there. But then an anatomist says, "Yes, there is an ATP reaction, but it is part of a yet larger picture. The ATP reaction is contracting a muscle attached to a vocal cord." Now this is when a neurologist shows up and says that the vocal cord is not being contracted arbitrarily. The muscle fibers are firing on the command of a nerve from the brain. And a musician says, "Now you are in my territory. The connected brain is creating music; a person is singing." But there is yet more. An economist arrives to say that it is always all about money. The person is singing for pay. But a sociologist chimes in, "Not so fast. The singer could have been singing for money elsewhere. The singer chose that spot because she is singing in the chorus with her friends." That's when the theologian notes that the choir is singing the "Hallelujah Chorus." They are worshiping God.

Human beings are intricately complex, living at multiple, interactive levels of reality. The physicist who describes underlying particle interaction may be quite accurate, but her description is far from complete. A summary at one level of the involved complexity may be correct without describing higher levels of complexity that are just as real, and yet not described by the lower level. If one uses the term *soul* to refer to a separate entity that initiates our personality and choices, or as an emergent phenomenon of the body, what we call soul is more than what could be diagrammed with a neurological chart. Whatever its genesis, there is more there, and it is deeply interconnected. When the body is tired, the soul finds it difficult to pray.

Reductionism is elegant, but impoverished. It so focuses on one aspect of the subject or event that it renders us blind to the rest of the connected reality. In 2005, Dean E. Hamer wrote a widely read book called *The God Gene: How Faith is Hardwired Into Our Genes*. A more accurate title would have been *A genetic sequence (VMAT) which may be associated with a tendency (<1%) toward an* *experience of perceiving self and non-self as one.* But that would not have sold as many copies. Genes play an important part in our formation and function, but only a part.

Genotype, the sum total of our genes, does not even determine all of our phenotype, what our body eventually comes to be. For example, identical twins have the same set of genes. They come from one embryo that has doubled. Yet their fingerprints will be different. The pattern of arch, tented arch, whorl, and loop will differ between them. If one identical twin develops type 1 diabetes, the chance of the other twin developing type 1 diabetes is about 50%. That is a much higher chance than for someone in the general population. Genes make a difference. But if type 1 diabetes was solely determined by genetic heritage, it would be 100%. One's genes influence if one will develop the disease, but do not alone determine that.

As to phenotype, which is deeply but not completely genetic, it is not all there is to being a particular human being. Two identical twins may look quite similar on the outside, while one becomes a carpenter and the other a chemist, one a Buddhist and the other a Baptist. We are deeply formed by our genes, but not destined by them. To the degree that our genes predestine us, that destiny is to have to make choices.

Genes and Human Choice

A worker ant has no choice. It will do the same behavioral program dictated by its genes whether on an ice flow or in the Amazon jungle. In contrast, retriever puppies, at a higher level of complexity, may override their genetic inclinations. If you present a retriever puppy with a body of water such as a lake, most likely it will jump in with glee to splash and swim about. A dachshund puppy on the same shore will show no interest. If it falls in the lake, it will sink like a rock and so be in immediate need of rescue. Yet as much as a retriever has the built-in genetic instructions to love and play with water, it can be trained to go in the water only when it hears a whistle or even to avoid the water. Dogs live at a level of complexity where they do not have to follow their genetic programming.

Now as a human being, you are more able than a dog. When you look in the refrigerator late at night, you may see a stalk of celery and a tub of ice cream. Which one looks more interesting? It is a safe guess you are most intrigued by the ice cream. Human beings have a built-in, genetic reward for eating fat. Fat tastes good. It is in that juicy steak or creamy ice cream. Preferring the taste of fat is a good strategy for living in a low calorie environment. When food is in short supply, seeking energy-rich fat is the quickest way to assure the calories that one needs. However, if one lives in an environment that is calorie rich and so one has already had the optimal number of calories for that day, the more healthy choice would be the celery. Anticipating the biological reward for consuming fat does not require that one has to do so. Human beings live at a level of complexity such that they can feel a genetic drive and choose to channel it, or even ignore it, to their benefit.

Here is another example. Mouse mothers have a gene called FosB. It gives them a biological reward when they hold still to nurse their pups. If that gene is missing, the mouse mother will not hold still to nurse her pups. Instead the mouse mother will keep her normal pattern of constant foraging for food, even to the point of the pups starving to death. The FosB gene gives behavioral instructions that are essential to passing on the mouse mother's genes. Human parents have the same FosB gene. It just feels warm and right to feed one's baby. Can a human parent who lacks that gene and its biological reward choose to feed his or her baby? Yes of course. Human beings make choices beyond genetic tendencies, even sometimes contrary to them.

Our genes influence our mental life, but they do not determine all of our bodies, let alone all our behavior. We can blindly follow our genetic tendencies, but it is well within our reach to encourage, resist, or channel our genetic drives and tendencies. Our genes usually encourage a course that has worked. That is no small benefit, but they do not definitively tell us what we *should* pursue. The clearest genetic marker for criminal violence is a Y chromosome. All males, and only males, have a Y chromosome. Females can act violently too, but they do so at a far lesser rate then those who carry a Y chromosome. That Y-chromosome tendency may be quite helpful to a warrior, politician, or entrepreneur, but it cannot be exercised indiscriminately. And simply because one carries a Y chromosome does not mean that one should be, or indeed will be, criminally violent. We human beings can choose what to do with our genetic behavioral tendencies.

Not everyone who is an alcoholic has known genes for alcoholism, but there are family lineages that carry genes that are strongly associated with alcoholism. However, we do not say, "You have genes that encourage alcoholism, so go, therefore, and be a good alcoholic." Inherited genes usually encourage behaviors that at past places and times have sometimes been helpful, but they are not foolproof guidance for the present or a trump card over other concerns. Simply having a genetic drive does not establish whether it should be carried out, nor if it should be, how or when. Some genetic tendencies should be encouraged. Some should be resisted. Some are fitting in one case and not another. Some are simply an aspect of one's personality.

So What Do We Do With Our Genetic Inclinations?

Charlotte Mason wrote into a world that was decidedly Christian in its convictions, and she affirmed the Christian faith at the heart of her work. Undoubtedly she would have been familiar with appeals to Psalm 139, where it is said that God "knit me together in my mother's womb" (NIV, 1973/2011). The context of that quote is a prayer of praise for God's knowledge and presence. The subject is not that one's genetic inheritance should be played out as it is. When a child is born with a cleft palate, they will not be able to speak or eat. We do not say, "God chose that you would have the genes for cleft palate, so it must be part of God's mysterious plan to build your character." On the contrary, it is the standard of care to take the child to surgery to correct that genetic condition. We live in the world, where things are often not the way they should be, and we correct them where we can. Ellen Dollar (2012) writes of her struggle with osteogenesis imperfecta. Often called brittle bone disease, the genetic condition renders her bones so fragile that they can snap at any moment, and do. Her femur breaking in two is just as painful and crippling as it would be for anyone else. Is it God's plan that she have that condition and pass it on to her children, or is that something to correct for her sake, and for her children, if we are able to?

Genes give us not so much a blueprint of how we should live, but a lay of the land. Your terrain may have a mountain to one side and a canyon to the other, but where you go on that landscape is still for the most part your choice. Or think of a sailboat. Your genes give you the condition and shape of the sails and the hull. The environment gives you the direction and intensity of the wind and currents. How you set the sails and rudder determines where you go. We have all seen people with sound sails and hulls, with the wind at their backs, who then steer in circles. We have also seen people with small sails and the wind against them who make amazing progress. Ultimately, the set destiny that our genes give us is to have choices.

We should follow some of our genetic tendencies, and not others. It is our responsibility to discern which is which and act accordingly. As Paul wrote in Romans 12:2, "Do not just reflect this world [or your genes], rather be transformed by the renewal of your mind so that you will live God's good, pleasing, and complete will for you" (author's translation). Our focus should be on the good and to enable the good and to become persons who naturally and freely choose the good. Our genes shape our physical body, behavior, and convictions, but we are sufficiently complex that we can decide which tendencies to listen to and how to manifest them. With that in mind, how can we help our children learn to discern, choose, and be well?

Different Notes in Harmony

The Christian tradition calls for all to grow in bearing the fruit of the presence of God's Holy Spirit. Such will be manifested in love, joy, peace, patience, goodness, deference, and self control, and is expected to develop wherever God reigns (Galatians 5:22). But while these traits are to be characteristic of all God's people, people yet come in all shapes and sizes. Gregory of Nazianzen (ca. 381) writes of James and John, "the sons of thunder, thundering the spirit" (Oration 41:14). Saul aggressively persuades, pursues, and cajoles to stamp out the early followers of Jesus and then becomes Paul, who spreads the Way of Christ with the same temperament. Followers of Christ are to reflect the image of Christ—to have a family resemblance—but also to each be unique individuals with particular callings. Along with these vocations come particular gifts for pursuing them, bestowed by God's choice and grace.

This should lead us to grace for one another. Some of the characteristics expected of all of us really are harder for one person than for another. Before becoming proud of one's own accomplishments, one should remember that some things actually are easier for one person than another, and some things are more challenging. Addictions, whether rooted in genes, experiences, or past choices, can be deeply resistant to change. Positive change for ourselves and others will often be incremental, requiring encouragement, and over time, requiring resolute compassion and patience. Growth in character is more of a marathon than a sprint, more like learning an instrument than a single song. The goal is for all to reflect God's presence and image, but not to be otherwise interchangeable parts. We have different skill sets and callings to serve one another. The ideal is not a unison of all singing the same note. The goal is the harmony of different notes rightly working together.

Mason's method of reading great books and narrating them lends itself well to variety, interest, comprehension, interpretation, and communication. It is understandable that she thought that the best education is to read great classic books and then tell their story "with power, clearness, vivacity and charm" (Mason, 1925/2008b, p. 54). There is much to commend in such an approach, and she can be quite focused on that one method, such as when she says "The only vital method of education appears to be that children should read worthy books, many worthy books" (Mason, 1925/2008b, p. 19). However, not every child is genetically endowed to learn that way. Some of us understand and retain quite well in a verbal format of reading and telling through words. But there are also those who need to move or manipulate, or to interact with a text in a group, or to see what they study in three dimensions. These approaches can be accommodated to some degree in a read and tell format. For example, the visual learner can make a chart of a book's argument, or a kinetic learner can pace as they read and act out a book's main point. In the pictured front page of *The Teacher's World*, Mason celebrates examples of what students can achieve when free to explore great books through their particular innate styles and skills. The differentiated learning movement has developed substantial insights and methods for making these connections (Tomlinson, 1999/2014; Reutzel & Cooter, 2000/2011; Kasten et al., 2005).

But some ways of learning are at loggerheads with Mason's method. The dyslexic starts with a genetic code that finds the written word an almost unbreakable code. I have

FIGURE 1

"The Week's Message" by Charlotte Mason in The Teacher's World,
March 4, 1914

Note. Original item at the Armitt Museum and Library, Ambleside,
England, UK. Image from Charlotte Mason Digital Collection at
Redeemer College, Ancaster, Ontario, Canada. Used by permission.

a daughter who is brilliant but, due to dyslexia, initially found words on the printed page to be gibberish. It took great effort on her part and that of her teachers, over an extended time, to break through. Not all do. Now she loves to read, did honors work throughout university, and is a licensed and experienced teacher in a public school system. People come prewired. All can learn. We should recognize each one's unique endowments and play as much as we can to their strengths.

How Does This Apply Specifically to Moral Education?

Developing the student's responsibility, self-motivation, and self-discipline that Mason emphasizes is helpful to all learning endeavors. These are indeed dispositions that will bless a lifetime of learning and action. Some will develop easily for a particular person, others not. Sometimes, ironically, the ones that develop with greatest difficulty may in that arduous process teach one of the most valuable virtues, a habit of committed effort over time. The truly great accomplishments only look easy because of the effort that has gone into developing them. One of the most important dispositions one can learn is to commit to the skill of ongoing, developing, practice. No one is simply born ready for great accomplishments. Assuming such condemns one to passivity that is not rewarded. One cannot change one's genes. One can change what one chooses to develop and practice. Learning to choose a goal and pursue it until it is achieved is one of the most important skills one can ever develop, and it is essential to the most valuable skills. It is said that the violinist Haifetz was once approached by a fan after a brilliant concert, who exclaimed, "I would give my life to play like you!" Haifetz of course replied, "I have."

The disposition to persist in a worthy process of development is a key virtue for education and the rest of life. Virtues are, after all, positive habits of perspective, initiative, and response. Attention is the ability to focus and the commitment/habit to focus on what most matters. The will then is where the student chooses thoughtfully and consistently, building a habit of attending to worthy purpose. (Mason, 1886/2008a, p. 214).

It is not enough to recognize what is right. One needs to train the will to seek to recognize what is right and then to pursue it. While recognizing what is right is important, it is not enough. The student needs "to distinguish between 'I Want' and 'I Will'" (Mason, 1905/1989b, Preface, Principle 15). It is easy to feel what one wants. What a person should do is to choose well that which one wills. I may want to sleep now, but I will to write this monograph. What one wills guides and motivates decisions and actions over time. This requires conscious evaluation and a pattern of wise choice that becomes a habit.

How does one choose well who to be? Mason (1925/2008b) saw certain "ineradicable principles" abiding in us, but was sure that our eyes must be taught to recognize them (p. 52). Her observation is akin to that of Paul in Romans 2:15 where he says that all people "show that the requirements of the law are written on their hearts, their consciences also bearing witness" (NIV, 1973/2011). Each person can flee these requirements, or reject them, or become so callous to them by neglect that they no longer come to mind, but they are there if one is honest with oneself.

These convictions can be uncovered by moral education. This is achieved most effectively by providing vocabulary and concepts to recognize, articulate, and practice them. An important approach to that end is reading lives widely, and evaluating the described choices, above all in the "storehouse of example and precept, the Bible" (Mason, 1925/2008b, p. 51). It is essential to remember in this process that whether in history, biographies, or Christian scriptures, one is not to duplicate every described action. We are not to emulate King David's adultery with Bathsheba and the murder of her husband Uriah. Every account is to be evaluated for insight into what one might get right and how one might go wrong. Granted, this learning to discern is a challenging skill of mind and heart that does not come easily to students or adults. Mason (1906/1989a) notes that "All youth are cocksure because they have not encountered yet, that equally reasonable and equally intelligent persons may hold opposite views on a question" (p. 321).

Mason sees reading widely to be the most effective course for understanding how people think and decide while consciously evaluating from a Christian perspective. She wrote to Sir Michael Sadler in 1901, "As for definite religious teaching, I think its aim should be that indicated in St John 17:3" (Mason, 1901, as cited in Kitching, 1952). That text reads "This is eternal life; that they know you, the only true God, and Jesus Christ, whom you have sent" (NIV, 1973/2011, Jn 17:3). She continues:

> Ethical teaching flows naturally from the study of the Gospels as also from that of the Old Testament and of the Epistles.... I have not tried the effect of a graded course of moral instruction on non-theological lines. Such a course seems to me unphilosophical and likely to result in persons whose virtues are more tiresome than their failings. (Mason, 1901, as cited in Kitching, 1952)

There are ethical systems that do not refer to God. Mason found such too easily misguided, even to the point of harm. She thought the most healthy and resilient ethics come from knowing Jesus Christ. For Mason, the best ethics motivation is "not from external threats" but rather from "joyful relationship with Jesus Christ" (Mason, 1901, as cited in Kitching, 1952). Such provides life-giving teaching, modeling, and empowered accompaniment.

Mason's child-centered education recognizes each child as a unique person. Remembering that, along with what we have learned from genetics, directs us to teach in a way that best connects with and works with each child's individual capacities and inclinations. The child's genes are formative, and so would best be taken into account. Yet they are not of themselves a set destiny. We have genuine choice in how we channel their influence, and so are able to consciously and conscientiously shape who we become. Whatever one's genetic heritage, the virtues of well-focused attention and self-motivation are worth recognizing, emulating, and practicing out of joyful relationship with the source of all that is good.

References

Dollar, E. P. (2012). *No easy choice: A story of disability, parenthood, and faith in an age of advanced reproduction.* Westminster John Knox Press.

Ebstein, R. P., Novick, O., Umansky, R., Priel, B., Osher, Y., Blaine, D., Bennett, E. R., Nemanov, L., Katz, M., & Belmaker, R. H. (1996). Dopamine D4 receptor (D4DR) exon III polymorphism associated with the human personality trait of novelty seeking. *Nature Genetics, 12*(1), 78–80. https://doi.org/10.1038/ng0196-78

Holy Bible, New International Version (NIV). (2011). Biblica. https://www.biblegateway.com/versions/New-International-Version-NIV-Bible/#booklist (Original work published 1973)

Kasten, W. C., Kristo, J. V., McClure, A. A., & Garthwait, A. (2005). *Living literature: Using children's literature to support reading and language arts.* Pearson/Merrill/Prentice Hall.

Kitching, E. (1952). Wait half a century. *Parents' Review. 63,* 300–315.

Lesch, K.-P., Bengel, D., Heils, A., Sabol, S. Z., Greenberg, B. D., Petri, S., Benjamin, J., Müller, C. R., Hamer, D. H., & Murphy, D. L. (1996). Association of anxiety-related traits with a polymorphism in the serotonin transporter gene regulatory region. *Science, 274*(5292), 1527–1531. https://doi.org/10.1126/science.274.5292.1527

Mason, C. M. (1914, March 4). The week's message. *The Teacher's World, X*(460), 1. (CMC Box 53, File 483, Modes 2017.1080). https://archive.org/details/Box-CM53FileCMC483/mode/1up

Mason, C. M. (1989a). *Formation of character.* Tyndale House. (Original work published 1906)

Mason, C. M. (1989b). *Ourselves: Improving character and conscience.* Tyndale House. (Original work published 1905)

Mason, C. M. (2008a). *Home education.* Wilder Publications. (Original work published 1886)

Mason, C. M. (2008b). *Towards a philosophy of education.* Tyndale House. (Original work published 1925)

Nazianzen, G. (n.d.). Oration 41:4. In C. Browne & J. Swallow (Trans.) Select orations of Saint Gregory Nazianzen. In P. Schaff & H. Wace (Eds.), *A select library of Nicene and Post-Nicene fathers of the Christian church* (Vol. VII, p. 384). Eerdmans. (Original work published ca. 381)

Reutzel, D. R., & Cooter, R. B. (2011). *Strategies for reading assessment and instruction: Helping every child succeed.* Pearson Education. (Original work published 2000)

Tomlinson, C. A. (2014). *The differentiated classroom: Responding to the needs of all learners* (2nd ed.). Association for Supervision & Curriculum Development. (Original work published 1999)

Appendix A

Mason's 20 Principles

1. Children are born *persons*.
2. They are not born either good or bad, but with possibilities for good and for evil.
3. The principles of authority on the one hand, and of obedience on the other, are natural, necessary and fundamental; but—
4. These principles are limited by the respect due to the personality of children, which must not be encroached upon, whether by the direct use of fear or love, suggestion or influence, or by undue play upon any one natural desire.
5. Therefore, we are limited to three educational instruments—the atmosphere of environment, the discipline of habit, and the presentation of living ideas. The P.N.E.U. Motto is: "Education is an atmosphere, a discipline, and a life."
6. When we say that "*education is an atmosphere*," we do not mean that a child should be isolated in what may be called a 'child-environment' especially adapted and

prepared, but that we should take into account the educational value of his natural home atmosphere, both as regards persons and things, and should let him live freely among his proper conditions. It stultifies a child to bring down his world to the 'child's' level.

7. By "education is a discipline," we mean the discipline of habits, formed definitely and thoughtfully, whether habits of mind or body. Physiologists tell us of the adaptation of brain structures to habitual lines of thought, *i.e.*, to our habits.

8. In saying that *"education is a life,"* the need of intellectual and moral as well as of physical sustenance is implied. The mind feeds on ideas, and therefore children should have a generous curriculum.

9. We hold that the child's mind is no mere *sac* to hold ideas; but is rather, if the figure may be allowed, a spiritual *organism*, with an appetite for all knowledge. This is its proper diet, with which it is prepared to deal; and which it can digest and assimilate as the body does foodstuffs.

10. Such a doctrine as *e.g.* the Herbartian, that the mind is a receptacle, lays the stress of Education (the preparation of knowledge in enticing morsels duly ordered) upon the teacher. Children taught on this principle are in danger of receiving much teaching with little knowledge; and the teacher's axiom is "what a child learns matters less than how he learns it."

11. But we, believing that the normal child has powers

of mind which fit him to deal with all knowledge proper to him, give him a full and generous curriculum; taking care only that all knowledge offered him is vital, that is, that facts are not presented without their informing ideas. Out of this conception comes our principle that,—

12. "*Education is the Science of Relations*"; that is, that a child has natural relations with a vast number of things and thoughts: so we train him upon physical exercises, nature lore, handicrafts, science and art, and upon *many living* books, for we know that our business is not to teach him all about anything, but to help him to make valid as many as may be of—

"Those first-born affinities

That fit our new existence to existing things."

13. In devising a SYLLABUS for a normal child, of whatever social class, three points must be considered:—

(*a*) He requires *much* knowledge, for the mind needs sufficient food as much as does the body.

(*b*) The knowledge should be various, for sameness in mental diet does not create appetite (*i.e.*, curiosity).

(*c*) Knowledge should be communicated in well-chosen language, because his attention responds naturally to what is conveyed in literary form.

14. As knowledge is not assimilated until it is reproduced, children should 'tell back' after a single reading or hearing: or should write on some part of what they have read.

15. A *single reading* is insisted on, because children have naturally great power of attention; but this force is dissipated by the re-reading of passages, and also, by questioning, summarising, and the like.

Acting upon these and some other points in the behaviour of mind, we find that *the educability of children is enormously greater than has hitherto been supposed*, and is but little dependent on such circumstances as heredity and environment.

Nor is the accuracy of this statement limited to clever children or to children of the educated classes: thousands of children in Elementary Schools respond freely to this method, which is based on the *behaviour of mind*.

16. There are two guides to moral and intellectual self-management to offer to children, which we may call 'the way of the will' and 'the way of the reason.'

17. *The way of the will*: Children should be taught, (*a*) to distinguish between 'I want' and 'I will.' (*b*) That the way to will effectively is to turn our thoughts from that which we desire but do not will. (*c*) That the best way to turn our thoughts is to think of or do some quite different thing, entertaining or interesting. (*d*) That

after a little rest in this way, the will returns to its work with new vigour. (This adjunct of the will is familiar to us as *diversion*, whose office it is to ease us for a time from will effort, that we may 'will' again with added power. The use of *suggestion* as an aid to the will *is to be deprecated*, as tending to stultify and stereotype character. It would seem that spontaneity is a condition of development, and that human nature needs the discipline of failure as well as of success.)

18. *The way of reason*: We teach children, too, not to 'lean (too confidently) to their own understanding'; because the function of reason is to give logical demonstration (*a*) of mathematical truth, (*b*) of an initial idea, accepted by the will. In the former case, reason is, practically, an infallible guide, but in the latter, it is not always a safe one; for, whether that idea be right or wrong, reason will confirm it by irrefragable proofs.

19. Therefore, children should be taught, as they become mature enough to understand such teaching, that the chief responsibility which rests on them as *persons* is the acceptance or rejection of ideas. To help them in this choice we give them principles of conduct, and a wide range of the knowledge fitted to them. These principles should save children from some of the loose thinking and heedless action which cause most of us to live at a lower level than we need.

20. We allow no separation to grow up between the intellectual and 'spiritual' life of children, but teach them that the Divine Spirit has constant access to their spirits, and is their continual Helper in all the interests, duties and joys of life. (Mason, 1925/2008d)

About the Author

James C. Peterson holds the endowed Schumann Chair in Christian Ethics at Roanoke College and serves on the faculty of the Virginia Tech Carilion School of Medicine as well. He is an ordained minister who has researched molecular and clinical genetics on grant from the National Institutes of Health (USA), and earned his PhD in ethics from the University of Virginia. He is the Editor-in-Chief of *Perspectives on Science and Christian Faith* (a peer reviewed journal celebrating its 75th year), and has been called to give expert testimony at the National Academy of Sciences (USA). He has served as president of the Canadian Scientific and Christian Affiliation. Both the American Scientific Affiliation and the International Society for Science & Religion (founded at Cambridge

University) have elected him as a Fellow. He and his wife homeschooled their children, and he has given plenaries at several Charlotte Mason conferences in the UK and the USA.

About the Charlotte Mason Institute

The Charlotte Mason Institute is a non-profit based in the USA that helps educators—through its curriculum, conferences, publications, ongoing research, training, and social media—to practice Charlotte Mason's relational education. Mason (1842-1923), a British educator and philosopher, designed, developed, and promoted a relational education in a living environment filled with books, experiences, nature, and ideas, where the child is viewed as a person and the educator as one who cooperates with God. The Institute engages current educational research and draws on Mason's design for education and her life work, which included authoring six volumes on education, establishing a parent's union, a teacher's college, an educator's journal, and a curriculum. In all its initiatives and collaborations, the Institute, founded almost twenty years ago, is committed to a vision of a relational education for all students and all educators in all settings.

About the Armitt Museum and Library

The Armitt is a museum, gallery and library in the UK which explores the stories and heritage of Ambleside, its people and the wider Lakeland world. Originally founded in 1912 by historian and naturalist Mary Louisa Armitt, it was set up as a subscription reference library and later expanded into collecting significant works from notable people as well as residents of Ambleside. Some of the collections include fungi paintings by Beatrix Potter, the Charlotte Mason archive, art by Kurt Schwitters, photography by Herbert Bell, the Abraham Brothers and Joseph Hardman, as well as archaeological material from the Ambleside Roman fort. In addition, there are thousands of books, articles and early publications relating to the history of the Lake District. The Armitt is a Trust and charity, open to visitors throughout the year for general interest, research, and events. Funds raised are used to ensure the museum can remain open for the benefit of all.

About the University of Cumbria

The University of Cumbria's Ambleside campus in the heart of England's Lake District is synonymous with Victorian educational pioneer Charlotte Mason. From 1984, Charlotte Mason's House of Education, was located at Scale How on the Ambleside campus. Over generations, the University continued to deliver higher education and teacher education with, depending on the era, alumni from Charlotte Mason College, Lancaster University, or St Martin's College before the University of Cumbria was formed in 2007. Today the University of Cumbria is a modern university transforming lives and livelihoods through its learning, applied research, and practice. The University's Learning, Education and Development (LED) research centre focuses on supporting practitioners to develop research-informed practice and publish research that has impact on policy and practice. The Ambleside Campus's Charlotte Mason Studies contributes to the University's three pillars of people, place, and partnerships by leading and participating in internationally collaborative research, writing, and convening that connects Charlotte Mason's legacy with education today. The program includes annual Scholar-In-Residence appointments, conferring of research fellowships on international scholars with expertise in Charlotte Mason, publications, and hosting conferences.

THE CHARLOTTE MASON CENTENARY MONOGRAPH SERIES

Elaine Cooper
The Powerful and Neglected Voice of Charlotte Mason: A Coherent, Holistic Approach to Education for Our Times

Prof. Hilary Cooper
Charlotte Maria Shaw Mason: Her place in the pantheon of educational theorists and her relevance today

Lisa Cadora, MA, and Esther Lightcap Meek, PhD
Knowing as Loving: Philosophical Grounding for Charlotte Mason's Expert Educational Insights

Deani Van Pelt, PhD, and Camille Malucci
Charlotte Mason's Great Recognition: A Scheme of Magnificent Unity

Elizabeth Millar, DPT Student
The Inherent Generosity within a Charlotte Mason Education and a Practical Theology of Joy

Emily Rodgers Bowyer, MSEd, and Brynn Dickie Bowyer, MA
A Feast of Living Ideas in a World of Bytes: Welcoming Charlotte Mason into the Digital Age

Douglas J. Sikkema
For the World's Sake: Charlotte Mason's Enduring Wisdom for the Anthropocene

David J. Chalcraft, PhD, Sally Elton-Chalcraft, PhD,
   Rebekah Ackroyd, PhD, and Helen Jones, BA
   *Reading Charlotte Mason's The Saviour of the World in
   Past
   and Present Contexts: Biblical Studies in the Classroom*

Professor Elliott Shaw, PhD
   *Engaging with Spirituality in the Classroom: Applying
   Charlotte Mason's Theological Anthropology to Current
   Educational Practice in a Secular Age*

Dr. Frances E. F. Ward
   *Charlotte Mason on the Abundant Life: Attention and
   Education for Character*

James C. Peterson, PhD
   *My Genes Made Me Do It! Moral Education, Charlotte
   Mason, and the New Genetics*

Prof. Lois Mansfield
   *Field Notebooks and Natural History Journals:
   Cornerstones of Outdoor Learning*

Jen Ager, MA, and Heather Prince, PhD
   *Charlotte Mason's Pedagogical Approach: Embedded
   Outdoor and Experiential Learning*

Dr. Adrian Copping
   *Engaging with Story to Engender Living Ideas: A 21st-
   century Charlotte Mason critique of teaching and assessing
   reading in the UK (and beyond?)*

Shannon R. Whiteside, PhD
   *Narration and Retelling: Charlotte Mason's Living
   Method of Learning*

J. Carroll Smith, EdD, with John Thorley, PhD
*Relational Educational Leadership: Critical Insights from
the Correspondence of Charlotte Mason and Henrietta
Franklin*

Jack Beckman, PhD
*From Continuance to Dissolution in a Post-Charlotte Mason
World: Four Principals' Experiences at Charlotte Mason
College (1923-1960)*

Deani Van Pelt, PhD, and Jen Spencer, BS, MA, EdD
*Students as Persons: Charlotte Mason on Personalism and
Relational Liberal Education*

Made in the USA
Columbia, SC
02 July 2024